TO: _____

FROM: _____

_____

_____

_____

POSITIVE ME

Journal

is a tool to help you keep all things POSITIVE about your
absopositively, wonderfully, uniquely made self in view.
There are 20 topics that will help you open your eyes and
remember who you are.

No pressure to complete all 10 (at 1st). Just jot things down
as they come to mind. And if you have a day when you start
doubting yourself, pick this journal up and
start flipping through the pages.

My hope and prayer is that you will eventually run
out of room and will need additional space on these pages.
You are so much more than you know.

- Sharli N. Berry, LPC

Don't Let What You Cannot
Do, Interfere With What
You Can Do.

- John Wooden

Things I Am Good At:

1
2
3
4
5
6
7
8
9
10

Is There Something In My Life That Makes Me Forget Time While I'm Doing It?

The Problem Isn't Your
Body, It's How You View
Your Body!

– *Sharli Berry*

What I Like About My Appearance:

1
2
3
4
5
6
7
8
9
10

If I Didn't Feel Shame or Fear, What Would I Do Now?

To Accomplish Great Things, We Must Not Only Act, But Also Dream; Not Only Plan, But Also Believe

– Anatole France

I Wish:

1 _____
2 _____
3 _____
4 _____
5 _____
6 _____
7 _____
8 _____
9 _____
10 _____

What Is My Biggest Dream? What Am I Doing to Accomplish it?

_____
_____
_____
_____
_____
_____
_____

Don't Live Down To
Expectations. Go Out
There And Do Something
Remarkable

- Wendy Wasserstein

I Have:

1 _____

2 _____

3 _____

4 _____

5 _____

6 _____

7 _____

8 _____

9 _____

10 _____

Am I Living According to the Expectations and Dreams of Others, or My Own? How Do I Distinguish Them From Each Other?

_____

_____

_____

_____

_____

_____

_____

Before You Think About
Quitting, Think About
Why You Started

– Sharli Berry

I Want:

1
2
3
4
5
6
7
8
9
10

What Motivates Me to Work Hard?

I Cannot Do All The Good
That The World Needs,
But The World Needs All
The Good That I Can Do

- Jana Stanfield

I've Helped Others By:

1 _____

2 _____

3 _____

4 _____

5 _____

6 _____

7 _____

8 _____

9 _____

10 _____

My Gift To the World is…..

_____

_____

_____

_____

_____

_____

_____

When You Are Able To Identify Your Values, Your Life Decisions Become Easier

- Sharli Berry

What I Value The Most:

1
2
3
4
5
6
7
8
9
10

How Do My Values Guide My Daily Decisions?

Being Challenged In
Life Is Inevitable, Being
Defeated Is Optional

- Roger Crawford

Challenges I Have Overcome:

1
2
3
4
5
6
7
8
9
10

What Is The Most Courageous Thing I Have Done? How Did I Feel Afterwards?

What Sets You Apart Can Sometimes Feel Like A Burden And It's Not. And A Lot Of The Time It's What Makes You Great.

-Emma Stone

Things That Make Me Unique:

1
2
3
4
5
6
7
8
9
10

In What Kinds of Things Am I Brilliant?

Whoever Is Happy Will
Make Others Happy Too

- Anne Frank

Times I've Made Others Happy:

1

2

3

4

5

6

7

8

9

10

What Makes Me Laugh the Most?

Many Of Life's Failures
Are People Who Did not
Realize How Close They
Came To Success When
They Gave Up.

- *Thomas Edison*

Skills I Have Acquired:

1 _____

2 _____

3 _____

4 _____

5 _____

6 _____

7 _____

8 _____

9 _____

10 _____

What Does it Take For Me to be Successful?

_____

_____

_____

_____

_____

_____

_____

_____

A Single Son Endowed
With Good Qualities Is Far
Better Than A Hundred
Devoid Of Them

- *Chanakya*

Positive Qualities I Possess:

1
2
3
4
5
6
7
8
9
10

What opportunities have I missed because I undervalued my positive qualities? How do I prevent it from happening again?

If You Think You Can
Or You Think You Can't,
Either Way You Are Right

– Anthony Robbins

Bad Things I Am Not:

1 _____
2 _____
3 _____
4 _____
5 _____
6 _____
7 _____
8 _____
9 _____
10 _____

Someday I hope I will be able to….

_____
_____
_____
_____
_____
_____
_____

God Created All Men Equal. Why Do Some Accomplish Far Greater Accomplishments Than Others? Because They Had A Vision, A Desire, And They Took Action

— Thomas J. Vilord

Small Positives I Am Discounting:

1
2
3
4
5
6
7
8
9
10

Am I Focusing More on What My Life Looks Like, Than What it Feels Like? Why?

A Time Comes When You Need To Stop Waiting For The Man You Want To Become And Start Being The Man You Want To Be

- *Bruce Springsteen*

I'm Grateful For:

1

2

3

4

5

6

7

8

9

10

How Often Do I Give Myself Permission to Enjoy Life? What Do I Need to Stop Doing so I Can Have More Time to Enjoy Life?

The Key To Achievement Is
Being A How Thinker, Not
An If Thinker

– Unknown

Things I Have Achieved, However Small:

1
2
3
4
5
6
7
8
9
10

What Have Been the Most Important Moments of Learning in My Life? What Have I Learned From Them?

When You Realize How
Powerful Your Thoughts
Are, You Would Never
Meditate on Another
Negative Thought

– Sharli Berry

Compliments I Have Received:

1 _____

2 _____

3 _____

4 _____

5 _____

6 _____

7 _____

8 _____

9 _____

10 _____

Would I Be Proud of Myself If I Spoke to Other People in the Same Way as My Thoughts Speak to Me? How Do My Thoughts Speak to Me?

_____

_____

_____

_____

_____

_____

_____

Evaluate The People In Your Life, Then Promote, Demote, Or Terminate

– Unknown

How A Person Who Cares About Me Might Describe Me:

1 _____

2 _____

3 _____

4 _____

5 _____

6 _____

7 _____

8 _____

9 _____

10 _____

What Kind of People or Situations Do I Attract? What Does That Say About Me?

_____

_____

_____

_____

_____

_____

_____

Somebody Is Always Doing
What Someone Else Said
Couldn't Be Done

– Unknown

What Other People Tell Me I'm Good At:

1
2
3
4
5
6
7
8
9
10

My purpose in life just might be....

If I Have The Belief That I
Can Do It,

I Shall Surely Acquire The
Capacity To Do It

Even If I May Not Have The
Capacity At The Beginning.

– Mahatma Ghandi

Aspects Of Myself That I Would Appreciate If They Were Aspects Of Another Person:

1 _____
2 _____
3 _____
4 _____
5 _____
6 _____
7 _____
8 _____
9 _____
10 _____

What expectations do I have for my life?

_____
_____
_____
_____
_____
_____
_____

Self-Beliefs That May Be Keeping Me From Reaching My Potential:
Write Positive Affirmation Underneath

1

   a

2

   a

3

   a

4

   a

5

   a

6

   a

7

   a

8

   a

9

   a

10

   a

What I ♥ About Me:

1
2
3
4
5
6
7
8
9
10
11
12
13
14
15
16
17
18
19
20